WHEN THE
DARKNESS
CLOSES IN

FINDING GOD'S LIGHT IN THE PROMISES OF HIS WORD

RICHARD KUENZINGER

innovo
PUBLISHING
innovopublishing.com

Published by Innovo Publishing, LLC
www.innovopublishing.com
1-888-546-2111

Innovo Publishing LLC is a Christ-centered publisher located near Memphis, TN. Since 2008, Innovo has published quality books, eBooks, audiobooks, music, screenplays, and online and physical curricula that support the Great Commission, equip believers, and help create a positive Christian worldview. Innovo's capabilities and global reach provide Christian authors, artists, and ministries access to the world for Christ. To learn more about Innovo Publishing, visit our website at innovopublishing.com. To connect with other Christian creatives and to learn best practices for creating, publishing, marketing, and selling Christian titles, visit the Christian Publishing Portal at cpportal.com.

WHEN THE DARKNESS CLOSES IN
Finding God's Light in the Promises of His Word

Copyright © 2025 by Richard Kuenzinger
All rights reserved.

No part of this publication may be reproduced, stored in a retrieval system, or transmitted in any form or by any means electronic, mechanical, photocopying, recording, or otherwise, without the prior written permission of the Author.

Unless otherwise noted, all scripture was taken from the Holy Bible, New International Version®, NIV® Copyright ©1973, 1978, 1984, 2011 by Biblica, Inc.® Used by permission. All rights reserved worldwide.

Scripture marked KJV was taken from the King James Version of the Bible. Public domain.

ISBN: 979-8-88928-148-1

Cover Design & Interior Layout: Innovo Publishing, LLC

Printed in the United States of America
U.S. Printing History
First Edition: 2025

This book is dedicated to mental health professionals, counselors, ministers, and chaplains. I also want to dedicate it to my friends—and your friends—who are willing to listen without passing judgment.

I want to thank Innovo Publishing, especially Rachael Carrington (editor) and Yvonne Parks (cover designer) for their support and encouragement.

Special thanks to my big brother in Christ, Butch Porch, for listening and sharing your experiences.

CONTENTS

Preface: A Snapshot of Mental Health ix
Introduction: Do Not Be Afraid to Talk About It xiii

JOB 15

NAOMI 27

DAVID 35

ELIJAH 49

JEREMIAH 57

JONAH 67

PETER 75

PAUL 85

JESUS 93

PUSH BACK THE DARKNESS 97

Afterword 101
Appendix 1: Crisis Response Numbers and Websites 103
*Appendix 2: Christian Responses to Loss of Spouse
   and/or Child* 105
More by Richard Kuenzinger 117

PREFACE:

A SNAPSHOT OF MENTAL HEALTH

—◦—

As believers, we are called to bear one another's burdens and extend compassion to those who are hurting. Mental and emotional struggles are more common than many realize, touching the lives of individuals and families both inside and outside the church. The following statistics—sourced from Johns Hopkins Medicine and the National Institute of Mental Health—highlight just how widespread these challenges are. As you will see, mental health affects most of us at some stage in our life. This information is shared not to alarm, but to remind us that many are silently suffering and in need of hope, healing, and the love of Christ through His people.

MENTAL AND BEHAVIORAL HEALTH[1]

According to the most recent data published by the National Institute of Mental Health (NIMH), a division of the National Institutes of Health, mental health conditions represent some of the leading contributors to disability in developed economies, including the United States and many other countries.

---

1. Johns Hopkins Medicine, "Mental Health Disorder Statistics," Johns Hopkins Medicine, accessed 2024, https://www.hopkinsmedicine.org/health/wellness-and-prevention/mental-health-disorder-statistics.

PREFACE: A SNAPSHOT OF MENTAL HEALTH

Among the most impactful conditions are major depressive disorder, bipolar disorder, schizophrenia, and obsessive-compulsive disorder.

In any given year, roughly one-quarter of adults in the United States—approximately 26 percent of individuals age 18 and older—experience a diagnosable mental health condition. Co-occurring disorders are common, with mood disorders frequently appearing alongside anxiety disorders or substance use disorders.

Each year, an estimated 9.5 percent of U.S. adults live with a depressive disorder, including major depression, bipolar disorder, or dysthymia. Major depression occurs nearly twice as often in women as in men, although bipolar disorder affects men and women at comparable rates. Major depressive disorder can develop at any stage of life, though initial onset most often occurs in the mid-twenties.

Bipolar disorder affects about 2.6 percent of adults annually, with first manic episodes typically emerging in early adulthood. Schizophrenia impacts approximately 1 percent of the U.S. population, usually appearing in late adolescence or early adulthood in men, and somewhat later—often in the twenties or early thirties—in women.

Most individuals who die by suicide have an identifiable mental health condition, most commonly a mood disorder or substance use disorder. While men die by suicide at significantly higher rates than women, women report more suicide attempts. The highest suicide rates in the United States occur among elderly White men over the age of 85, though suicide remains one of the leading causes of death among adolescents and young adults between the ages of 15 and 24.

Anxiety disorders are also widespread, affecting approximately 18 percent of adults between the ages of 18 and 54 each year. These disorders include panic disorder, obsessive-compulsive disorder (OCD), post-traumatic stress disorder (PTSD), generalized anxiety disorder (GAD), and various phobias. Panic disorder often begins in late adolescence or early adulthood, while symptoms of OCD commonly emerge during childhood or the teenage years. GAD can develop at any point in life, though risk is highest from childhood through middle age. Individuals with OCD frequently experience additional challenges such as depression, substance use disorders, or eating disorders. Social anxiety disorder typically begins early, often during childhood or adolescence.

Understanding the scope, complexity, and prevalence of mental health conditions is essential for reducing stigma, promoting early intervention, and encouraging compassionate care. These statistics serve as a sobering reminder that mental illness affects people from all walks of life and at every stage—from childhood through old age. By fostering awareness and supporting evidence-based treatment, we can create environments where those struggling are more likely to seek help, find hope, and experience healing.

INTRODUCTION:

DO NOT BE AFRAID TO TALK ABOUT IT

When I was younger, there was a stigma attached to people who had mental health problems. I do not believe the health care profession fully understood the long-term effects of mental health in those days. We have had some type of therapists and clergy since the days of Job. Some of these provided good advice, and some did not.

Looking back at my younger days, I realize that people were embarrassed to admit that they were struggling mentally; I know I was. Men were considered weak, and women were thought to be overly emotional if they admitted to a problem.

How many people suffered physically, mentally, and emotionally because they could not get the help they needed? How many suicides could have been prevented if someone would have validated the struggle? A good friend or counselor should be able to help you find a reason to live (see Appendix 1 for helplines).

For all the problems that surrounded the COVID-19 pandemic, one bright spot was the greater recognition of our mental health needs. Of course, COVID-19 also exasperated the problem, but there was a greater awareness to "check on our people."

INTRODUCTION: DO NOT BE AFRAID TO TALK ABOUT IT

Let's walk through Scripture and look at people who struggled with their mental health. We will not look at every case in the Bible, but these are a few who have impacted my faith walk. We will attempt to look at their struggle and how they got through it.

My hope is that you will find guidance and comfort in your own struggle. I always tell people that they need someone to talk to—someone to whom they are not related and whom they can trust. Do not be afraid to talk about how you are feeling or what you are going through.

I also hope and pray that you will find the strength to trust in God in the darkness and allow His light to guide you through it. The Bible never promised us that following Jesus would be easy, but we do have the promise that He will never leave us. *He is present with you in your darkness.*

Chapter 1

JOB

WHY JOB?

We are beginning our study through Scripture with the book of Job because it is here where we have a glimpse of what is happening in the world that we cannot see or even begin to understand. It is here where we see that the God of all creation allows suffering even for those who love Him. It is in the book of Job where we see the purpose of suffering: to recognize Who God is and draw near to Him.

> ¹ Then Job replied to the Lord:
>
> ² "I know that you can do all things;
>   no purpose of yours can be thwarted.
> ³ You asked, 'Who is this that obscures my plans without knowledge?'

> *Surely I spoke of things I did not understand,*
> *things too wonderful for me to know.*
>
> ⁴ *"You said, 'Listen now, and I will speak;*
> *I will question you,*
> *and you shall answer me.'*
> ⁵ ***My ears had heard of you***
> ***but now my eyes have seen you.***
> ⁶ *Therefore I despise myself*
> *and repent in dust and ashes."*
>
> —JOB 42:1-6

How many times have you heard a sermon about Job? If someone is going through hard times, we are quick to refer to Job. We talk about the "patience of Job." However, how often do we think about and talk about his mental health?

I want to encourage you to read the entire book of Job—but do not read it one chapter at a time. Do not read a chapter today and another tomorrow. Try reading it in its designed segments. For example, when Job is speaking, read the entire speech. Chapters 6 and 7 are the words of Job, so read them together. I think you will get a better idea of what is happening if you read it this way.

We need to see that God allows suffering for a reason. I believe the reason, or purpose, is different for each of us, but it is safe to say that the primary purpose of our suffering, mentally or physically, is to draw us nearer to our God.

WHAT DO WE KNOW ABOUT THE MAN JOB?

> *¹ In the land of Uz there lived a man whose name was Job. This man was blameless and upright; he feared God and shunned evil. ² He had seven sons and three daughters, ³ and he owned seven thousand sheep, three thousand camels, five hundred yoke of oxen and five hundred donkeys, and had a large number of servants. He was the greatest man among all the people of the East.*
>
> —Job 1:1-3

We know that Job was rich, he was righteous, and he was respected. "He was the greatest man among all the people of the East." He had a big family and a lot of stuff. In our culture today, we would say that Job was "blessed."

Job feared God and he shunned evil, and verse 5 tells us that he had a custom of praying for his children, just in case they had sinned against God. Suffice it to say, Job had a strong foundation for his faith walk.

This is something we should all consider: how strong is our faith when everything is going well? I believe that Job was ready when disaster came because his faith was not based on an hour in a church on Sunday.

If you want to learn about a person's faith, watch how they respond under stress, or how they respond to a tragedy. Today, some people will ask you, "What good is all that time you spend in church trying to be a good person when your God still allowed the tornado to destroy your house? Why bother?" These types of questions are nothing new. Job's wife asked the same thing in a different way:

> *His wife said to him, "Are you still maintaining your integrity? Curse God and die!"*
>
> —JOB 2:9

Job did maintain his integrity:

> *He replied, "You are talking like a foolish woman. Shall we accept good from God, and not trouble?"*
>
> —JOB 2:10

As you read the rest of the story, you will see that Job was not happy about what had happened, nor was he happy with the "comfort" his friends provided—but he never turned against God.

WHAT TRAUMATIC EVENTS LED TO JOB'S MENTAL HEALTH CRISIS?

Allow me to put this in today's vernacular: first some foreigners came and stole his animals that he needed for work and killed most of the workers; then the sky exploded and killed the animals that he used for clothing and killed most of the workers; then another group of foreigners came and took all of the animals that he used for transporting his goods and also killed those workers;

and then a tornado hit the place where his kids were, and it killed everyone except one man.

What would you do? At what point would you curse the God you say you love?

However, Job did something that many people today would say was weird: he *worshiped*. Job fell down and worshiped his God.

> [20] *Then he fell to the ground in worship* [21] *and said:*
>
> *"Naked I came from my mother's womb,*
> *and naked I will depart.*
> *The* Lord *gave and the* Lord *has taken away;*
> ***may the name of the*** Lord ***be praised."***
>
> [22] *In all this, Job did not sin by charging God with wrongdoing.*
>
> —Job 1:20b-22

If you suffered through only one of these events, could you worship the God you say you follow? What if your loved one has brain cancer? What if your child was killed in a school shooting? What if you watched your family get swept away in a flood? Would you have the faith to say, "May the name of the Lord be praised"?

This was not the end of Job's pain—it was only the beginning. In chapter 2, Job lost his health. The greatest man in all the East was now unrecognizable by his closest friends.

When they saw him from a distance, they could hardly recognize him.

—Job 2:12

"... may the name of the Lord be praised."

—Job 1:21b

JOB'S MENTAL HEALTH CRISES

Then Job took a piece of broken pottery and scraped himself with it as he sat among the ashes.

—Job 2:8

Job had lost everything, and then he was afflicted with painful sores from his head to his feet. Why was he sitting in the ashes, scraping himself with a piece of pottery? What was going through his mind besides how much pain he was in?

His wife told him to get it over with, to "curse God and die." His friends sat nearby, but they did not say anything for seven days. I do not want to speculate about what Job was thinking, but how would you feel in this situation? Lonely, depressed, or worse—would you want to end your life? Your kids are gone, your livelihood is gone, your spouse is "so over it," and your friends are silent. Obviously, the people Job loved would not dress his wounds, so he sat in the rubble, in the ashes, and scraped himself.

Many commentaries agree that Job would have smelled very bad, and by using a piece of pottery, Job could scrape the boils and blisters to relieve the pus buildup. It sounds nasty—uncomfortable and painful.

Allow me to add another perspective as we consider current definitions of depression, trauma, and loneliness. This is by no means a clinical diagnosis of a man who lived more than three thousand years ago; this is only a hypothesis based on my experience and research.

Non-suicidal self-injury, or NSSI, is what people do to inflict physical pain upon themselves in order to relieve another pain—be it mental or physical. I have seen young people do this instead of seeking help.

I am not saying that Job was suicidal, but as we continue to read, we see that he wished he had never been born.

> *"Why did I not perish at birth,*
> *and die as I came from the womb?"*
>
> —Job 3:11

> *"Or why was I not hidden away in the ground*
> *like a stillborn child,*
> *like an infant who never saw the light*
> *of day?"*
>
> —Job 3:16

Job complained to God,

> ¹³ *"When I think my bed will comfort me*
> *and my couch will ease my complaint,*

> ¹⁴ *even then you frighten me with dreams*
>   *and terrify me with visions,*
> ¹⁵ *so that I prefer strangling and death,*
>   *rather than this body of mine.*
> ¹⁶ *I despise my life; I would not live forever.*
>   *Let me alone; my days have no meaning."*
>
> —Job 7:13-16

One of the questions my counselors always ask me is, "Do you ever go to sleep and hope you don't wake up?" My response last time was, "I go to sleep and don't want to deal with tomorrow, but I don't want to be dead."

Job preferred death and for God to leave him alone. These are the words of someone in crisis, someone who is hurting, and someone who needs another person to listen to them.

Chapters 4–37 are a running conversation between Job and his friends. This is a very common discussion you may hear when counseling someone in a time of suffering. I recommend every chaplain, counselor, and minister be familiar with this conversation because you will hear these questions and accusations often—questions about sin, righteousness, justice, and the holiness of God are often asked after a traumatic event.

WHERE DID JOB FIND COMFORT?

As we study the Scriptures, especially those portions that deal with suffering and mental health, we need to learn how to find comfort when our own darkness closes in. The last chapters of Job reveal to us a lesson that we need to hold onto in our own periods of darkness. God overwhelmed Job with the truth of Who He is.

In chapters 38–41, God Almighty revealed Himself to Job. He did not give Job a video to watch or a cute story to read; rather, God Almighty, the Creator of the universe, the only One Who controls your heartbeat— He revealed Himself to Job by explaining Himself.

Job did not see the Person of God standing in front of him, but he *saw* with understanding the Lord Almighty. Look at the words of Job:

> [1] *Then Job replied to the Lord:*
>
> [2] *"I know that you can do all things;*
> *no purpose of yours can be thwarted.*
> [3] *You asked, 'Who is this that obscures my plans without knowledge?'*
> *Surely I spoke of things I did*
> *not understand,*
> *things too wonderful for me to know.*
>
> [4] *You said, 'Listen now, and I will speak;*
> *I will question you,*
> *and you shall answer me.'*
> [5] ***My ears had heard of you***
> ***but now my eyes have seen you.***
> [6] *Therefore I despise myself*
> *and repent in dust and ashes."*
>
> —JOB 42:1-6

Job confessed that he had heard of God, but now, in the midst of his suffering and pain, he *saw* God Almighty.

It was in the words of God where Job saw Him. It was because of the words of God that Job repented and found comfort. Through all of Job's suffering, trauma, and depression, it was in the Word of God that Job *saw* God, as the Creator explained Himself to this man, Job. Romans 10:17 tells us that faith comes from hearing the Word of God.

There is no guarantee that when we turn to God in our suffering, He will bring immediate healing and prosperity. Please do not see that here. Instead, I want you to see that in your darkness you can turn to the Word of God for comfort.

In the same way that God went to Job in his pain, this same God has come to us in the Person of Jesus the Messiah, and He has revealed Himself to us in His Word (John 1:18). If you have access to *this* little book, you also have access to *His* Book, the Holy Bible.

The same holds true for us. When we are hurting, we can see our God in His Word, and that is where we need to begin our search for comfort. As we counsel our friends, the Word of God is where we need to begin our counseling.

> *³ Praise be to the God and Father of our Lord Jesus Christ, the Father of compassion and the God of all comfort, ⁴ who comforts us in all our troubles, so that we can comfort those in any trouble with the comfort we ourselves receive from God. ⁵ For just as we share abundantly in the sufferings of Christ, so also our comfort abounds through Christ. ⁶ If we are distressed, it is for your comfort*

> *and salvation; if we are comforted, it is for your comfort, which produces in you patient endurance of the same sufferings we suffer.*
>
> —2 Cor 1:3-6

Christians will suffer—mentally, physically, and spiritually—and our Lord knows it. Only in Christ will we find true comfort. It took me a long time to realize this truth.

HOW CAN YOU HELP SOMEONE WHO HAS BEEN THROUGH PROLONGED SUFFERING, TRAUMA, DEPRESSION, AND HOPELESSNESS?

If you want to help someone through a difficult time, just be there. Be present where they are, and allow yourself to enter into their place of hurting.

Job's friends were there with him, but I do not know how much they really helped. In Job 13:14, he called them "worthless physicians." Makes me think they were not very helpful.

Be present—not on your phone, and not thinking about what to say. Listen more than you speak, and do not be afraid to say, "I don't know," when they ask the *why* questions.

Chaplains and ministers practice the *ministry of presence*. Being there is more important than what you say. You do not need to speak. Sometimes your silent presence is enough. As you are able, help them find comfort in the Word of God. Use the light of God's Word to help your friend begin to push back the darkness.

Chapter 2

NAOMI

WHY NAOMI?

Naomi is an important individual to study because I think that we, as the church, quickly forget about the struggles of our widows and single parents.

According to the book of Ruth, as far as we know, Naomi did not lose everything in a short span of time as Job did; however, that doesn't mean she didn't experience trauma of a different kind. I teach my chaplain students that trauma is defined by the survivor's perception—not by how it appears to an outsider or even a counselor. What feels deeply traumatic to one person might seem insignificant to someone else.

We could focus solely on the fact that Naomi was a widow and a mother of two sons, living in a foreign country around 1100–1050 B.C. That alone was probably traumatic.

WHAT DO WE KNOW ABOUT NAOMI?

Naomi is only spoken of in the book of Ruth, which is set in the period of the Judges. She and her husband were Ephrathites from Bethlehem, also known as Ephrathah (Ruth 1:2). There was a famine in Israel, and Naomi and her family traveled to the east side of the Jordan to the area of Moab to survive. This is a fifty-mile journey, which crosses the Jordan River and some mountainous terrain. On foot, the trip could take seven to ten days.

Naomi made this trip twice—the first time with her husband and sons, and the return trip with only her daughter-in-law, Ruth.

WHAT TRAUMATIC EVENTS LED TO NAOMI'S MENTAL HEALTH CRISIS?

Elimelech and Naomi had two sons, but Elimelech died while they were living in Moab. Their sons married Moabite women, and after ten years, the sons died, leaving their mom and their wives childless.

By the end of the first four verses in Ruth chapter 1, this woman who had been forced to leave her home with her husband and two sons because of a famine, is now a widowed refugee with two foreign daughters-in-law.

> *. . . and Naomi was left without her two sons and her husband.*
>
> —RUTH 1:5B

Can you feel the despair in the writer's pen?

In our study of the book of Job, it appeared that everything happened in a relatively short time span. However, the tragic events in Naomi's life were spread over a period of at least ten years, maybe a little more.

One tragedy is enough to push most people into some sort of depressive or anxious state. Naomi was a refugee, then a widow, and then childless. In the culture of that time, her situation appeared hopeless. Her situation seemed desperate.

NAOMI'S MENTAL HEALTH CRISES

We do not know about Naomi's life before the famine, but where the Bible is silent, we should be as well.

After fleeing to a foreign land to help her family to survive, Naomi later faced another tragedy—her husband died, leaving her a widowed refugee with two sons and their wives. Though life continued in Moab, there remained hope that one day they would return to Bethlehem together as a family.

Have you ever been forced to move away from your homeland? Even in the twenty-first century, every year people across Central America, Africa, the Middle East, and Eastern Europe are being forced to flee from their countries because of war or famine. Today, millions of people are displaced.

(Widows often experience depression, grief, and loneliness. They may be angry at their deceased spouse for leaving them, and some may feel that they would be better off dead—see Appendix 2.)

Ten years later, while still living in Moab, Naomi's sons died. She was now not only a refugee in a foreign land and widowed, but she was now childless—except for her two foreign daughters-in-law. Naomi was depressed and hopeless, and she felt abandoned by God.

Look at what she told her daughters-in-law:

> [12] *"Return home, my daughters;* **I am too old to have another husband.** *Even if I thought there was still hope for me—even if I had a husband tonight and then gave birth to sons—* [13] *would you wait until they grew up? Would you remain unmarried for them? No, my daughters.* **It is more bitter for me** *than for you, because* **the Lord's hand has turned against me!***"*
>
> —RUTH 1:12-13

We can feel Naomi's grief every time she speaks in the first chapter. She expressed her pain to those who greeted her when she returned to Bethlehem:

> [20] *"Don't call me Naomi,"* [meaning "pleasant"] *she told them. "Call me Mara,* [meaning "bitter"] *because the Almighty has made my life very bitter.* [21] *I went away full, but the* LORD *has brought me back empty. Why call me Naomi? The* LORD *has afflicted me; the Almighty has brought misfortune upon me."*
>
> —RUTH 1:20-21

Psychologists tell us there are five stages of grief. Most psychologists and counselors refer to the first stage of grief as *denial*. Some include *numbness*. I have talked to survivors and first responders after a traumatic event who do not feel anything. They are in shock or numb.

We do not know if Naomi suffered from traumatic memories, nightmares, or numbness, but we do know that she suffered stress, anxiety, depression, and bitterness, and she felt abandoned by God:

> *"The Almighty has made my life very bitter.*
> *. . . the Almighty has brought misfortune upon me."*

How was she even able to walk the fifty miles back to Bethlehem in this mental state?

As she made her return journey, she did not walk home alone. . . .

WHERE DID NAOMI FIND COMFORT?

In Ruth 1:6, although not explicitly defined as "comfort," I believe she found solace in the knowledge that "the Lord had come to the aid of his people by providing food for them." Naomi knew it was time to go home, where she would no longer be a refugee.

Naomi found comfort in the love of Ruth. May the Lord God give every one of His hurting children someone like Ruth.

> *¹⁶ But Ruth replied, "Don't urge me to leave you or to turn back from you. Where you go I will go, and where you stay I will stay. Your people will be my people and your God my God. ¹⁷ Where you die I will die, and there I will be buried. May the Lord deal with me, be it ever so severely, if even death separates you and me."*
>
> —Ruth 1:16-17

Naomi found comfort among her people, where she was no longer a foreigner. She found comfort in Ruth's love and companionship, knowing that she did not need to go through her physical and emotional journey alone.

We must remember that at this time, Ruth was also a childless widow with her own grief. However, Ruth knew about the people of Naomi—and the God of Naomi—and in this knowledge, Ruth found her strength.

> *"Your people will be my people and your God my God."*

Naomi also found comfort in the promise of God—the Kinsman Redeemer.

> *An uncle or a cousin or any blood relative in their clan may redeem them. Or if they prosper, they may redeem themselves.*
>
> —Lev 25:49

> *"The Lord bless him!" Naomi said to her daughter-in-law. "He has not stopped showing*

> *his kindness to the living and the dead." She added, "That man is our close relative; he is one of our guardian-redeemers."*
>
> —RUTH 2:20

So the woman who asked to be called "Mara" because she was bitter found comfort in the reality of the Word of God. She found comfort among the people of God, and she found comfort as she walked with someone who loved her and her God.

During our struggles and our crises, we cannot always see the hand of God in our lives. Naomi was hurting and feeling hopeless. When the famine came to Bethlehem, she did not know that the day was coming when she would hold the baby boy who would become the grandfather of King David, from whom the Messiah would come. In her suffering, she did not have the *big picture* of God's perfect plan.

> *[14] The women said to Naomi: "Praise be to the LORD, who this day has not left you without a guardian-redeemer. May he become famous throughout Israel! [15] He will renew your life and sustain you in your old age. For your daughter-in-law, who loves you and who is better to you than seven sons, has given him birth."*
>
> —RUTH 4:14-15

HOW CAN YOU HELP SOMEONE WHO IS STRUGGLING WITH GRIEF AND DEPRESSION?

How can we minister to someone who is walking through this type of struggle? From the questionnaire in Appendix 2, the common answer is, "Show compassion—not just in words but with your time and prayers, and help them become active in helping others."

In every traumatic event, our response should be the same: be present. It is the ministry of presence that brings comfort in suffering.

Naomi needed to be around her people, and she needed someone to walk with her. She also needed to be reminded of the promises of her God. We should be able to comfort those around us in the same way, if we only trust in the power of the Holy Spirit working in us to give us the wisdom that we need.

> *Religion that God our Father accepts as pure and faultless is this: to look after orphans and widows in their distress and to keep oneself from being polluted by the world.*
>
> —JAMES 1:27

Chapter 3

DAVID

WHY DAVID?

If you are familiar with the life of David in the Bible, you are probably thinking, *Of course David is on this list!*

When I read about David in the Psalms, 1 and 2 Samuel, and 1 Chronicles, I see a man who struggled in many ways and a man who walked with God.

We could build a chapter around Saul, the king who preceded David, because he had a lot of mental health issues, but the focus of this book is to discuss people who found comfort and healing in the Word and work of God. Saul did not do that. Saul was disobedient to the Lord God, even to the point of consulting a medium—whom some translations refer to as the "witch of Endor" (1 Sam 28:3-25).

Saul is not a good example of someone who dealt with his issues in a God-honoring way. David, on the other hand, turned to the Lord time and time again. David wrote seventy-three of the psalms, and we can see his struggle and his path to healing in his writings. This chapter will focus on some of those psalms.

WHAT DO WE KNOW ABOUT DAVID?

David was from the tribe of Judah and the great-grandson of Boaz and Ruth. (He was a descendant of Naomi.) He was the youngest of seven sons of Jesse of Bethlehem. He was also a shepherd.

David was a musician and a warrior. He played the harp, and he killed a lion, a bear (1 Sam 17:34-36), and a giant named Goliath.

For all his greatness, David was also a sinner like all of us. He was an adulterer, a murderer, and a liar. However, David, unlike Saul, turned to the Lord in his failures, and it was in the presence of God where he found his salvation and hope.

We also know that David was chosen by God to lead the nation of Israel, and the eternal King of Kings would come from David's line. Paul said this about David:

> *After removing Saul, he made David their king. God testified concerning him: "I have found David son of Jesse, a man after my own heart; he will do everything I want him to do."*
>
> —ACTS 13:22

WHAT TRAUMATIC EVENTS LED TO DAVID'S MENTAL HEALTH CRISES?

David was anointed king while Saul was still on the throne, and for the remainder of Saul's life, he tried to kill David. So David was always running and hiding from Saul (1 Sam 19:11; 1 Sam 21–25).

David fought animals and very large men (1 Sam 16–18). He was betrayed by his son Absalom, who killed his half-brother Amnon to avenge the rape of their sister Tamara, David's daughter (2 Sam 13:14-29). Absalom was later killed in battle (2 Sam 18:14-15).

David also lost a newborn son as a punishment from God for his sins against Uriah and Bathsheba (2 Sam 12).

The story of David shows us that even a king, even someone chosen and loved by God, will face difficulties, hardships, and struggles. David's story alone is a slap in the face to the prosperity (false) gospel.

Fear, anxiety, and depression were some of the struggles that David faced in his lifetime.

DAVID'S MENTAL HEALTH CRISES

There are countless books and articles about David's struggles—just do an internet search on "King David's mental health struggles" and you will find a lot of information. I recommend that you take some time to read the Psalms if you want to learn more about David's mental health struggles and how he found comfort.

In this chapter, I want to focus on his feelings and expressions, and I want to look at what he did to find help with prolonged depression, fatigue, fear, and anxiety.

As you read the Psalms of David, I want you to see how they begin with a struggle or a problem, and by the end of the psalm, David has recognized the greatness of God. David works from despair to praise. For many people, including myself, we have a tendency to enter into despair and stay there, without recognizing the work of God in our lives.

David found comfort in his writing as he poured out his grief and his praise to God. He cried out to God, and he remembered the love of God and the work of God, and in those times of remembering, he was able to worship again. Here, in the Word of God, David found his comfort, and I hope you will too.

Let's look at the *struggle* and the *comfort* together by reviewing some of David's psalms.

David recognized his need for the Lord:

> *Answer me when I call to you,*
> *my righteous God.*
> *Give me relief from my distress;*
> *have mercy on me and hear my prayer.*
>
> —Ps 4:1

David asked for relief, and then he said,

> *In peace I will lie down and sleep,*
> *for you alone, LORD,*

> *make me dwell in safety.*
> —Ps 4:8

In the presence of his God, David slept in peace. Do you wonder sometimes if the Lord hears you? David often cried to the Lord to hear him:

> *¹ Listen to my words, Lord,*
>   ***consider my lament.***
> *² Hear my cry for help,*
>   *my King and my God,*
>   *for to you I pray.*
> —Ps 5:1-2

David used the term *refuge* often. It conveys the idea of being in a place of security.

> *But let all who take refuge in you be glad;*
>   *let them ever sing for joy.*
> —Ps 5:11A

In distress he cried for help:

> *Lord my God, I take refuge in you;*
>   *save and deliver me from all who pursue me.*
> —Ps 7:1

> *The Lord is a refuge for the oppressed,*
>   *a stronghold in times of trouble.*
> —Ps 9:9

May we be able to take refuge in the stronghold of the Lord.

In his distress, David was able to sing praise to God Most High, *El Elyon*:

> I will give thanks to the LORD because of
> his righteousness;
>   I will sing the praises of the name of
> the Lord Most High.
>
> —Ps 7:17

The constant threat of his enemies took a toll on David's mental health:

> [13b] Have mercy and **lift me up from the gates of death**,
> [14] that I may declare your praises
>   in the gates of Daughter Zion,
>   and there rejoice in your salvation.
>
> —Ps 9:13b-14

Do you ever feel as though the Lord has abandoned you or has left you alone in your darkness?

> Why, LORD, do you stand far off?
>   Why do you hide yourself in times of
> trouble?
>
> —Ps 10:1

We may feel as though the Lord is far away, but He is not; He is near.

> You, LORD, hear the desire of the afflicted;
> you encourage them, and you listen to
> their cry.

—Ps 10:17

A beautiful example of pain and praise is found in Psalm 13. Four times David asks, "How long?" Do you get frustrated or feel hopeless when it seems that God is not moving?

> ¹ *How long, LORD? Will you forget me forever?*
> *How long will you hide your face from me?*
> ² *How long must I wrestle with my thoughts*
> *and day after day have sorrow in my heart?*
> *How long will my enemy triumph over me?*
>
> ³ *Look on me and answer, LORD my God.*
> *Give light to my eyes, or I will sleep*
> *in death,*
> ⁴ *and my enemy will say, "I have*
> *overcome him,"*
> *and my foes will rejoice when I fall.*

—Ps 13:1-4

I personally feel the pain in David's questions. *How long will I feel forgotten? How long will You hide from me? How long will I struggle with my thoughts?* (Being alone with my thoughts is my biggest struggle. If I have too much free time, I will begin to dwell on the past.) These questions are very real for anyone who struggles with their mental health.

Look at David's hope in Psalm 13 as he closes his prayer:

> *⁵ But I trust in your unfailing love;*
> *my heart rejoices in your salvation.*
> *⁶ I will sing the LORD's praise,*
> *for he has been good to me.*
> —Ps 13:5-6

Before David could become king, he had to survive the threat of Saul. After Saul was removed, David wrote Psalm 18—a psalm of praise. I want to highlight two verses in this Psalm.

> *In my distress I called to the LORD;*
> *I cried to my God for help.*
> *From his temple **he heard my voice**;*
> *my cry came before him, into his ears.*
> —Ps 18:6

David had cried for help, and he knew that he had been heard. Oh, may the Lord give me that kind of confidence!

Even in our darkness, light is available to us:

> *You, LORD, keep my lamp burning;*
> ***my God turns my darkness into light.***
> —Ps 18:28

David called Him "my God." He had a personal relationship with the only One who could bring him hope.

Let me reiterate: David was not perfect, nor was he sinless. He made a lot of bad choices, and some of them, I believe, led to some of his depression. When we sin, we are separated from God our Father, and that separation is mentally, spiritually, and physically painful.

We live in a time when many counselors avoid addressing sin in a person's life. Instead, they focus on other issues and simply encourage clients to think positive thoughts. David knew that his sin separated him from the Lord God. He cried out for mercy from God, and he rejoiced in the salvation of God.

I am not seeking to diminish the role of counselors and chaplains—they are valuable, especially when we need someone to talk to who isn't emotionally connected to us. But more than anything, what we truly need is to be in a right relationship with our Creator. That begins with recognizing that our sin has separated us from Him, and only through faith in the redeeming work of Jesus can we be restored to fellowship with God. That is the truth of the gospel of Jesus the Messiah.

With that in mind, let us look at Psalm 27:

> *The Lord is my **light and my salvation**—*
> *whom shall I fear?*
> *The Lord is the stronghold of my life—*
> *of whom shall I be afraid?*
> —Ps 27:1

When we are in a right relationship with God the Father, we have nothing to fear. This doesn't mean we won't face hardship or suffering—but it does mean He will be our strength in the midst of it.

> *⁷ Hear my voice when I call, LORD;*
> *be merciful to me and answer me.*
> *⁸ My heart says of you, "Seek his face!"*
> *Your face, LORD, I will seek.*
> *⁹ Do not hide your face from me,*
> *do not turn your servant away in anger;*
> *you have been my helper.*
> *Do not reject me or forsake me,*
> *God my Savior.*
>
> —Ps 27:7-9

David begged for mercy, he sought the "face" of his God, and he recognized his Savior, the only One who could save him for eternity.

This is a good time to mention that the salvation I am talking about in this book is *eternal salvation*. I am not talking about someone getting out of a hard place today, only to be there again next week. The salvation of God is His work in our lives that gives us hope in the darkness, understanding that the pain is temporary and He is eternal. His salvation of our souls has no end date.

David knew, and my prayer is that you also will know, the confidence of the salvation of God, and in that confidence that you, too, will experience the presence of God in your life now—today.

> *¹³ I remain confident of this:*
> *I will see the goodness of the LORD*

> *in the land of the living.*
> *14 Wait for the* LORD;
> *be strong and take heart*
> *and wait for the Lord.*
>
> —Ps 27:13-14

We often find David calling to the Lord for mercy. Psalm 30 is David's plea for mercy and his song of praise as he dedicated the temple plans:

> *10 Hear,* LORD, *and* **be merciful to me;**
> LORD, *be my help."*
>
> *11* **You turned my wailing into dancing;**
>   *you removed my sackcloth and* **clothed me with joy,**
> *12* **that my heart may sing your praises and not be silent.**
>   LORD *my God, I will praise you forever.*
>
> —Ps 30:10-12

I want to look at one more psalm of David. It is not easy to read because it speaks to the painful impact of sinful choices and the pain we suffer until the Lord God saves and restores us. So, we read Psalm 51, which David wrote after he had sinned with Bathsheba, killed her husband, and then lost the baby who was conceived in their affair:

> *1 Have mercy on me, O God,*
>   *according to your unfailing love;*
> *according to your great compassion*

> blot out my transgressions.
> ² Wash away all my iniquity
>   and cleanse me from my sin.
> ³ For I know my transgressions,
>   and my sin is always before me.
> ⁴ Against you, you only, have I sinned
>   and done what is evil in your sight;
> so you are right in your verdict
>   and justified when you judge.
>
> —Ps 51:1-4

Notice that David did not make an excuse for his sin; he acknowledged that he had sinned against God. He begged for mercy from the only Judge who could truly pardon him (and us). Only this Judge can bring restoration.

> ¹⁰ Create in me a pure heart, O God,
>   and renew a steadfast spirit within me.
> ¹¹ Do not cast me from your presence
>   or take your Holy Spirit from me.
> ¹² Restore to me **the joy of your salvation**
>   and grant me a willing spirit, to sustain me.
>
> —Ps 51:10-12

David asked to be made new *from the inside*, and this is what we all need when we sin—to be made a new creation. Salvation from God does not mean turning over a new leaf and trying to be a better person. To truly be saved, we need to surrender our lives to God and allow Him to make us new creations from the inside out (John 3:16-17; Acts 4:12; 2 Cor 5:17; 1 John 1:9).

> *⁹ If you declare with your mouth, "Jesus is Lord," and believe in your heart that God raised him from the dead, you will be saved. ¹⁰ For it is with your heart that you believe and are justified, and it is with your mouth that you profess your faith and are saved. ¹¹ As Scripture says, "Anyone who believes in him will never be put to shame." ¹² For there is no difference between Jew and Gentile—the same Lord is Lord of all and richly blesses all who call on him, ¹³ for, "Everyone who calls on the name of the Lord will be saved."*
>
> —Rom 10:9-13

These are only a handful of David's psalms. I encourage you to spend time in the book of Psalms daily, and allow the Word of God to do the work of God in your life both when you are in the darkness *and* when you are in the light.

HOW CAN YOU HELP SOMEONE WHO IS STRUGGLING WITH DEPRESSION AND ANXIETY?

One of the hardest things for me when walking with someone through trauma is staying silent. I often want to share that I've suffered too—but that's usually not helpful. When someone is hurting, what they need most is for you to listen. There may come a time to share your own experience—or that time may never come. In moments of grief, *it's not about you.*

We spent a lot of time with David. We didn't cover everything, but we looked at these verses because David is a wonderful example of finding hope and comfort in the presence of God.

Someone may ask you, *Where is this God you are talking about?* Or, they may question the reality of God. A time of grief and trauma is not the time for spiritual debate. For David, the presence of God was His Word. The same is true for us today. The same God who spoke to David will also speak to us, if we will allow Him to speak.

You may have five days, or you may have five minutes with someone. You need to be prepared to help them find comfort in the Bible—the Word of God. Find one or two psalms that speak to you in your darkness, and when you are with someone you can say, "May I show you where I have found comfort?"

When you feel all alone, you are not alone. The God of all creation hears our prayers.

> *Do not be anxious about anything, but in every situation, by prayer and petition, with thanksgiving, present your requests to God.*
>
> —Phil 4:6

Chapter 4

ELIJAH

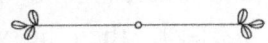

WHY ELIJAH?

Elijah was a man of God—sent by God, with a mission from God. Today, we also have men and women of God who have been sent out by God with a mission. Elijah is a reminder for us that just because we are in ministry doesn't mean we are exempt from mental health crises and problems.

James 5:17 tells us that Elijah was a person just like us. He is a good example for us as we remember that in our depression, fatigue, anxiety, and loneliness, our God knows where we are, and we are not alone.

WHAT DO WE KNOW ABOUT ELIJAH?

Elijah was from Tishbeh in Gilead, and he was a prophet. His name means "my God is the Lord." We do not have a lot of information about his background, but what we do know can be found in 1 Kings 17–19 and 21, and 2 Kings 1–2.

Elijah served during the time of evil King Ahab in the northern kingdom of Israel. His ministry seemed to be a continuous challenge to Ahab and the people of Israel to turn from their wickedness and return to the true God.

The first thing Elijah did in his ministry was confront Ahab with the prophecy of a drought—and bringing bad news to the king is not a good way to begin your ministry (1 Kgs 17:1-7). Then he went into hiding where he was fed by ravens and drank from a brook, and eventually he went to another country where he was fed by a widow and her son (1 Kgs 17:8-16).

Elijah's next confrontation during the drought was with King Ahab and the prophets of Baal. He called down fire from heaven, defeating them all—which made Queen Jezebel furious (1 Kgs 18:17-40).

The rain finally came (1 Kgs 18:41-46) after the false prophets were cooked, but Elijah went into a deep depression (1 Kgs 19:1-18). He had participated in a great event, but nothing changed among the people, and the queen wanted him dead.

WHAT TRAUMATIC EVENTS LED TO ELIJAH'S MENTAL HEALTH CRISIS?

Elijah prophesied that there would be no rain for a few years, and then the Lord told him to go into hiding. The Lord told Elijah that the ravens would feed him, and the brook would provide water, and Elijah did as the Lord commanded (1 Kgs 17:5).

At first glance this does not seem so bad: do what God tells you, and He will take care of you. It is easy—until it is not easy. The brook dried up, and the ravens stopped coming.

Then the Lord told Elijah to go to another country because He had directed a widow there to take care of him. First, the Lord told birds to feed Elijah, and then he told a foreign, non-Jewish woman to feed him.

Everything was good until the Lord told Elijah to return to his land and confront Ahab *again* (1 Kgs 18:1). He was also returning to the queen who was killing the Lord's prophets and still wanted to kill Elijah.

Apparently none of these other prophets had confronted the king and queen about their evil practices.

> *Then Elijah said to them,* "***I am the only one of the Lord's prophets left****, but Baal has four hundred and fifty prophets.*"
> —1 Kgs 18:22a

Here, in this mountaintop experience, facing overwhelming odds while doing the will of God, Elijah felt alone.

The Lord worked a great miracle through Elijah and destroyed hundreds of bad guys, which is great in the movies but not so great when the queen wants you dead in real life. He was then on the run again, away from Jezreel.

THE MENTAL HEALTH CRISES OF ELIJAH

There was a time when Elijah felt as if he were the only one who cared and the only one working for the Lord. Have you ever had that feeling? You can be surrounded by people and at the same time feel alone. Have you ever felt as if you were the only one in your class or your workplace who cared? Are you involved in ministry and sometimes wonder, *Where is everyone? Why am I the only one left?*

In 1 Kings 19:4, after a mountaintop experience, Elijah was so depressed and afraid that he begged the Lord to let him die:

> *³ Elijah was afraid and ran for his life. When he came to Beersheba in Judah, he left his servant there, ⁴ while he himself went a day's journey into the wilderness. He came to a broom bush, sat down under it and **prayed that he might die**. "**I have had enough,** L*ORD*," he said. "**Take my life**; I am no better than my ancestors." ⁵ Then he lay down under the bush and fell asleep.*
>
> —1 K*GS* 19:3-5

Can you hear him screaming, *I have had enough!*—? In the light of the purpose of this book, that's how I am reading these verses. I can hear the defeated cry in the prophet's voice because I have cried the same. *No one cares! No one wants to go! No one is praying! No one is serving! No one is helping! I'm the only one!* These are words that I have said in my own struggle and in my own times of self-pity. What about you?

Elijah was tired. Depression, stress, and trauma all lead to fatigue. He was tired, and he laid down under a bush and fell asleep. Then, the Lord met him at what was likely his lowest point.

WHERE DID ELIJAH FIND COMFORT?

The Lord had been with Elijah from the beginning of his ministry, through the famine, on the mountain of burning false prophets, and now in this point of great despair. The Lord was always near.

> *⁵ Then he lay down under the bush and fell asleep.*
>
> *All at once an angel touched him and said, "Get up and eat." ⁶ He looked around, and there by his head was some bread baked over hot coals, and a jar of water. He ate and drank and then lay down again.*
>
> *⁷ The angel of the Lord came back a second time and touched him and said, "**Get up and eat, for the journey is too much for you**." ⁸ So he got up and ate and drank. Strengthened by that food, he traveled forty days and forty nights until he reached Horeb, the mountain of God.*
>
> —1 Kgs 19:5-8

The Lord knows where we are, what we have been through, and what we need for the work ahead. Why do we not turn to Him immediately in our sorrow? He is near, and He has not left us to walk alone, even when we feel alone. Look here:

> ⁹ᵇ **And the word of the Lord came to him:** "What are you doing here, Elijah?"
>
> ¹⁰ He replied, "I have been very zealous for the Lord God Almighty. The Israelites have rejected your covenant, torn down your altars, and put your prophets to death with the sword. **I am the only one left**, and now they are trying to kill me too."
>
> —1 Kgs 19:9b-10

When Elijah was spiritually and physically depleted, the "word of the Lord came to him." When Elijah got alone with God and blocked out all the storms so that he could hear the whisper, he found comfort in the Word of God. God told him,

> "Yet I reserve seven thousand in Israel—all whose knees have not bowed down to Baal and whose mouths have not kissed him."
>
> —1 Kgs 19:18

Elijah was not alone. He found his comfort in the presence of God, and he found the strength to carry on. The Word of God is the presence of God in our lives as well. Elijah's work was not finished just because he was ready to quit. God strengthened him because the journey was going to be long, and Elijah continued to do the work that the Lord had given him.

HOW CAN YOU HELP SOMEONE WHO IS STRUGGLING WITH DEPRESSION, FATIGUE, ANXIETY, AND LONELINESS?

I will say it again, and I will say it in every chapter: be there, be present, be available. We do not need to know why something happened or why someone is hurting; we only need to be available to listen.

Ministers or laborers can often fall into discouragement or even depression when they feel like they're the only ones doing the work. This usually happens when we shift our focus away from God's calling and start fixating on ourselves or comparing our efforts to others. Spiritually and emotionally, that kind of comparison is dangerous. I've heard people say, "Why can't we get more people from the church to help?" However, we are not responsible for what other people are doing with their own calling—we're only accountable for our own obedience.

We need to remember that God is working through others, not just us—and our focus should remain on what He has specifically called us to do. If you want to support someone who is struggling, especially someone in ministry, help them recognize God's presence through His Word.

Chapter 5

JEREMIAH

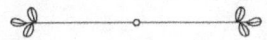

WHY JEREMIAH?

Why not Jeremiah? He is known as the *weeping prophet*, and it was not because he was happy-go-lucky. Think about this: Jeremiah saw the destruction of Jerusalem (Jer 6 and 52), the destruction of the Temple (Jer 52:13), and the destruction of his people as he watched them go into exile (Jer 52:24-30). He had every reason to be depressed.

That is why we need to look at the life of Jeremiah.

WHAT DO WE KNOW ABOUT JEREMIAH?

Jeremiah was a prophet in the southern kingdom of Judah before it fell to the Babylonians. He served as a prophet from the days of Josiah through the reigns of Judah's last four kings (Jer 1:2-3), and he died in 570 BC.

> *"See, today I appoint you over nations and kingdoms to uproot and tear down, to destroy and overthrow, to build and to plant."*
>
> —JER 1:10

He was called to take a message of wrath and destruction to the people of Judah, but he also had a message of hope. Jeremiah was told that it was going to be hard, and the people would not listen to him—but God was with him.

> *"They will fight against you but will not overcome you, for I am with you and will rescue you,"* declares the LORD.
>
> —JER 1:19

Jeremiah told the people that the captivity would *only* be seventy years (Jer 25:11; Dan 9:2). This was a glimmer of hope that the exiles had a timeline, and their Babylonian captors would be destroyed.

Jeremiah, with his scribe Baruch, is credited with the book of Jeremiah and the book of Lamentations.

WHAT TRAUMATIC EVENTS LED TO JEREMIAH'S MENTAL HEALTH CRISIS?

Jeremiah was hated by his people because he brought a message of destruction to them (Jer 11:21-23). No one wanted to hear that they were living in sin, nor did they want to hear that God was going to judge them. The same is as true today as it was back then.

He was beaten by order of one of the priests, a man who should have been aware of God's judgment.

> *¹ When the priest Pashhur son of Immer, the official in charge of the temple of the LORD, heard Jeremiah prophesying these things, ² he had Jeremiah the prophet **beaten and put in the stocks** at the Upper Gate of Benjamin at the LORD's temple.*
>
> —JER 20:1-2

Jeremiah was obedient to stand in the courtyard and tell everyone about the disaster that was coming, and then he was attacked.

> *But as soon as Jeremiah finished telling all the people everything the LORD had commanded him to say, the priests, the prophets and all the people seized him and said, "You must die!"*
>
> —JER 26:8

In chapter 37 he was thrown into prison, and then in chapter 38 he was thrown into a well. He was finally rescued by a foreigner who worked in the palace, but his own people had left him to die.

Jeremiah—commonly referred to as *the weeping prophet*— was also sentenced to work alone. The Lord forbade him to marry, and he walked this path of obedience for forty years with only the Lord at his side.

As I write this, I wonder how long I would have lasted in this situation. Jeremiah was told to take a message of judgment to his own people—who would not listen and even try to kill him. All along, he would have no one but God to share his pain with.

THE MENTAL HEALTH CRISES OF JEREMIAH

Loneliness, depression, social isolation, and physical suffering were all a part of Jeremiah's life as a prophet. We have talked about the beating he suffered as well as his arrest; now we are going to break down more of chapter 20 because I think it encapsulates the feelings he had regarding his circumstances.

> *⁷ **You deceived me, Lord, and I**
> **was deceived;***
>   *you overpowered me and prevailed.*
> ***I am ridiculed all day long;***
>   ***everyone mocks me.***
> *⁸ Whenever I speak, I cry out*
>   *proclaiming violence and destruction.*
> *So the word of the Lord has brought me*
>   *insult and reproach all day long.*
> *⁹ But if I say, "I will not mention his word*
>   *or speak anymore in his name,"*
> ***his word is in my heart like a fire,***
>   *a fire shut up in my bones.*
> *I am weary of holding it in;*
>   *indeed, I cannot.*
> *¹⁰ I hear many whispering,*
>   *"Terror on every side!*
>   ***Denounce him! Let's denounce him!"***
> *All my friends*

> are waiting for me to slip, saying,
> "Perhaps he will be deceived;
> then **we will prevail over him
> and take our revenge on him.**"
>
> —JER 20:7-10

Jeremiah was a good man, but he was still only a man. He was called by God to go to the people of God, and yet he felt "deceived." Some translations say "seduced." It was as if he knew this mission from God was a good one, but he did not realize the pain involved.

Do you get a sense that he was angry with God in verse 7? Have you ever been angry with God when you walked according to His plan, and it was painful?

I have heard people say, "The safest place to be is in the will of God." I say, *No, it is not.* The will of God is not always safe, nor easy, and oftentimes it is painful. However, walking in the will of God is walking *with Him* in obedience.

Instead of proclaiming the Word of God and seeing people repent, Jeremiah was attacked, ridiculed, and isolated. His friends were waiting for him to make a mistake so that they could destroy him. I think they wanted to destroy his reputation *and* destroy him physically. If he fell in regard to the Law of God, he would be put to death.

In the next chapter we will look at the story of Jonah—in many ways a huge contrast in character from Jeremiah. Unlike Jonah, Jeremiah could not *not* speak the Word of

God. Jeremiah's very soul was on fire with the message of God, and he could not keep it inside.

Can you imagine his stress? He knew that when he spoke it would not be received well, and if he chose not to speak it would be a huge problem as well.

The Apostle Paul had a similar feeling:

> *Woe to me if I do not preach the gospel!*
> —1 Cor 9:16b

Like Job, Jeremiah cursed the day of his birth. He knew God was with him, yet he was still suffering:

> *¹⁴ Cursed be the day I was born!*
>   *May the day my mother bore me not*
> *be blessed!*
> *¹⁵ Cursed be the man who brought my father*
> *the news,*
>   *who made him very glad, saying,*
>   *"A child is born to you—a son!"*
> *¹⁶ May that man be like the towns*
>   *the Lord overthrew without pity.*
> *May he hear wailing in the morning,*
>   *a battle cry at noon.*
> *¹⁷ For he did not kill me in the womb,*
>   *with my mother as my grave,*
>   *her womb enlarged forever.*
> *¹⁸* **Why did I ever come out of the womb**
>   **to see trouble and sorrow**
>   **and to end my days in shame?**
>
> —Jer 20:14-18

Why was I born to watch suffering, pain, and people hurting? Why do men and women and children who profess to know and love the Lord God have to suffer and watch others suffer? Why?!

Have you heard these questions before? Have you asked these questions yourself? The simple answer is that we live in a fallen world—a world marked by sin and suffering. This world is not going to change until the Lord returns. Of course, when someone is hurting, this is not the answer they want to hear.

It is time to take a moment and consider this question: *Why was Jeremiah born?* God had a plan for him, and that plan involved him taking the Word of God to the people. That is the same plan the Lord has for all of us today. The message is the same, and we have been saved and called to deliver this message to the people of the world—many of whom will reject it.

Sin separates us from a holy God, and if we do not submit to Him by turning from our ways to follow Him, then we will be eternally separated from Him. The message of the gospel is not always popular, but we have a command to deliver it to everyone. We also have the promise that the Lord is with us always.

> "... *teaching them to obey everything I have commanded you. And surely* **I am with you always**, *to the very end of the age."*
> —Matt 28:20

WHERE DID JEREMIAH FIND COMFORT?

Jeremiah knew the call of the Lord on his life. It was in the Word of God where Jeremiah experienced the presence of God, and in His presence, Jeremiah was able to walk alone—although he knew that he was never *really* alone.

> ⁴ The word of the LORD came to me, saying,
>
> ⁵ "Before I formed you in the womb I knew you,
>   before you were born I set you apart;
>   I appointed you as a prophet to the nations."
>
> ⁶ "Alas, Sovereign LORD," I said, "I do not know how to speak; I am too young."
>
> ⁷ But the LORD said to me, "Do not say, 'I am too young.' You must go to everyone I send you to and say whatever I command you. ⁸ **Do not be afraid of them, for I am with you and will rescue you**," declares the LORD.
>
> —JER 1:4-8

The words of God sustained him:

> When your words came, I ate them;
>   they were my joy and my heart's delight,
> for I bear your name,
>   LORD God Almighty.
>
> —JER 15:16

In the middle of his cries of pain and complaint in chapter 20, Jeremiah knew that the Lord was with him:

> **But the LORD is with me** *like a*
> *mighty warrior;*
> *so my persecutors will stumble and not*
> *prevail.*
> —Jer 20:11

HOW CAN YOU HELP SOMEONE WHO IS STRUGGLING WITH LONELINESS, DEPRESSION, SOCIAL ISOLATION, AND PHYSICAL SUFFERING?

The ministry of presence is something that everyone needs to learn and experience. If you want to help someone like Jeremiah, then be with them, listen to their story, pray with them, and lead them into the Word of God to find their comfort and strength.

We must all realize that some of us may walk through pain for a long period of time, as Jeremiah did, and others may experience temporary pain. We may not even find the relief we desire in this lifetime. For example, Jeremiah went into captivity with his people.

Remember that the Lord is with us, and the comfort we need is in His Word. He is an ever-present help in our time of need.

> [1] *God is our refuge and strength,*
> *an ever-present help in trouble.*
> [2] *Therefore we will not fear, though the earth*
> *give way*

> *and the mountains fall into the heart of the sea,*
> *³ though its waters roar and foam*
> *and the mountains quake with their surging.*
>
> —Ps 46:1-3

Chapter 6

JONAH

WHY JONAH?

Jonah is an interesting study. His depression was likely self-inflicted because of his sinful disobedience to God's call on his life.

Depression leads to fatigue, irritability, sleep problems, loss of interest in work or hobbies, anger, aggression, and oftentimes substance abuse.

I want to use this thought regarding depression as the lens through which we study Jonah, a man who was not excited about his mission.

WHAT DO WE KNOW ABOUT JONAH?

Jonah was from a small village north of Nazareth in the land of Zebulun. He lived during the days of Jeroboam II, King of Israel, from 782–753 BC. The book of Jonah is the only book with a message focused entirely on the Gentiles.

Jonah was sent to the Ninevites in Assyria with a message to repent or be destroyed. He did not want to take the message to them because he did not want to see them saved.

> *¹ But to Jonah this seemed very wrong, and he became angry. ² He prayed to the LORD, "Isn't this what I said, LORD, when I was still at home? That is what I tried to forestall by fleeing to Tarshish. I knew that you are a gracious and compassionate God, slow to anger and abounding in love, a God who relents from sending calamity.*
>
> —JONAH 4:1-2

Are we like Jonah? Do we avoid taking God's message to people whom we do not like because we know that God will save them? Shame on us!

Jonah was a real person, and Jesus used him as an example when the Pharisees asked for a sign:

> *³⁸ Then some of the Pharisees and teachers of the law said to him, "Teacher, we want to see a sign from you."*
>
> *³⁹ He answered, "A wicked and adulterous generation asks for a sign! But none will be given it except the sign of the prophet Jonah. ⁴⁰ For as Jonah was three days and three*

> nights in the belly of a huge fish, so the Son of Man will be three days and three nights in the heart of the earth."
>
> —MATT 12:38-40

WHAT TRAUMATIC EVENTS LED TO JONAH'S MENTAL HEALTH CRISIS?

It must be said that Jonah's sin led to the traumatic events recorded in his book. Let us not gloss over that fact and think this story is about a big fish. His situation is not like Job's, Naomi's, Jeremiah's, or Elijah's. He was blatantly disobedient to God; yet praise God for meeting him in his fallenness!

We see Jonah's depression clearly at the end of the book. We can also see his anger and self-pity, possibly even thoughts of taking his own life.

Have you ever hated the events in your life so much that you said something like, "I wish I was dead!" or, "I would rather be dead than do that!" What did you actually mean when those words left your lips? Likely, it was pure frustration speaking. (Of course, if you are counseling someone who says something like this, you need to take it seriously and ask some probing questions to be sure that they are only speaking out of frustration—see Appendix 1.)

So Jonah was told to go to the people he hated, and this mission made him angry with God. So he ran. But we cannot run from God, and we cannot avoid His call on our lives (Isa 46:10-11).

As Jonah was fleeing God's call, he was caught in a storm at sea. He confessed his sin of disobedience, and he testified to the greatness of the God he served. It's interesting to think that Jonah did not want to go to the pagans of Nineveh, yet here he was testifying to pagan sailors.

> ⁹ He answered, "I am a Hebrew and **I worship the LORD, the God of heaven, who made the sea and the dry land.**"
>
> ¹⁰ This terrified them and they asked, "What have you done?" (They knew he was running away from the LORD, because he had already told them so.)
>
> —JONAH 1:9-10

Jonah ended up being thrown off the ship and into the sea, then swallowed by a fish that was sent by the Lord—and the darkness closed in on Jonah.

THE MENTAL HEALTH CRISES OF JONAH

Jonah 1:4b tells us that Jonah had gone below deck, and he fell into a deep sleep during a severe storm. That sounds like fatigue to me, which is a sign of depression. At first glance, we can easily say that Jonah was comfortable running from God. However, based on what we know from his response in chapter 4, he was likely in the pit of depression. He was so determined to *not* go to the Gentiles that he was running to the ends of the earth to avoid his mission.

When we are in sin and running from God, it creates emotional and physical fatigue within our depressed state. Jonah was suffering from fatigue, depression, anger, and self-pity, and a large part of these feelings returned after he spent three days and nights in a large sea creature.

How angry do we have to be to forget about God's salvation by continuing to harbor bitterness toward someone created in God's image? Jonah was happy to be saved, but he was not happy when God saved the people Jonah hated.

Sometimes, in depression and anger, we want to give up and quit.

> *"Now, LORD, take away my life, for it is better for me to die than to live."*
>
> —JONAH 4:3

Again, I won't go so far as to say that he was ready to take his own life, but I think he was ready to give up.

> *⁸ᵇ He wanted to die, and said, "It would be better for me to die than to live."*
>
> *⁹ But God said to Jonah, "Is it right for you to be angry about the plant?"*
>
> *"It is," he said. "And I'm so angry I wish I were dead."*
>
> —JONAH 4:8B-9

He became furious because the plant the Lord had provided to shade him died. I know, you are probably thinking, *He wants to die.* Maybe, yes—maybe, no. I can't accurately clinically diagnose anyone, but I have many years of experience talking to people who are going through various types of trauma, and I truly believe that Jonah was *very* angry here.

It's possible that he wished he were dead, but he didn't actually want to take his own life. I have personally had times in my life when I was so depressed that I wished I were dead, but I did not actually want to die. I just did not want to be in that situation anymore. In a way, you could say that "I would be okay if tomorrow didn't come" (see reply #7 in Appendix 2).

WHERE DID JONAH FIND COMFORT?

> *¹ From inside the fish Jonah prayed to the L*ORD *his God. ² He said:*
>
> **"In my distress I called to the L**ORD **,**
> **and he answered me.**
> *From deep in the realm of the dead I called*
> *for help,*
> *and you listened to my cry.*
> *³ You hurled me into the depths,*
> *into the very heart of the seas,*
> *and the currents swirled about me;*
> *all your waves and breakers*
> *swept over me.*
> *⁴ I said, 'I have been banished*
> *from your sight;*
> *yet I will look again*
> *toward your holy temple.'*

> *⁵ The engulfing waters threatened me,[b]*
> *the deep surrounded me;*
> *seaweed was wrapped around my head.*
> *⁶ To the roots of the mountains I sank down;*
> *the earth beneath barred me in forever.*
> *But you, LORD my God,*
> *brought my life up from the pit.*
> *⁷ "When my life was ebbing away,*
> *I remembered you, LORD,*
> *and my prayer rose to you,*
> *to your holy temple.*
>
> *⁸ "Those who cling to worthless idols*
> *turn away from God's love for them.*
> *⁹ But I, with shouts of grateful praise,*
> *will sacrifice to you.*
> *What I have vowed I will make good.*
> *I will say, 'Salvation comes from*
> *the LORD.'"*
>
> —JONAH 2:1-9

Jonah's comfort, even in the belly of the fish, was found in his God. He knew that his God was near enough to hear him when he cried out. If the Lord God heard Jonah's cry from inside a fish, in the Mediterranean Sea, he will hear your cry from wherever you are in your darkness.

In his distress, Jonah called to the Lord, and the Lord answered. Jonah chapter 2 is a summary of his distress and his comfort. The "seaweed was wrapped around [his] head," but the Lord saved him when the darkness closed in on him.

The God of all creation provided for Jonah's salvation. This same God has also provided for our salvation. The God of Jonah will meet us in our fallenness too. He will not leave us in the darkness if we will turn to Him and cry out to Him in faith.

HOW CAN YOU HELP SOMEONE WHO IS STRUGGLING WITH DEPRESSION, ANGER, AND SELF-PITY?

If we do not spend time listening to people who are hurting, we will never realize the depth of their despair. Spend some time with someone who is going through a crisis, and allow them to share their feelings. Pay attention to their behavior, words, and actions. And give them the freedom to be silent. This is part of the ministry of presence. Do not take their silence to be your cue to talk. In the silence, it is best to remain quiet as well.

After a traumatic event, I always encourage the survivor to get help from a trained counselor. If you do not know how to connect someone to a counselor, they can text HOME to 741741. This will connect them with a trained crisis counselor, and they are available anytime, 24/7.

There is also an app available called "A Friend Asks." It contains questions to ask and resources to use to help someone who may be at risk of self-harm.

Finally, but most importantly, use the Word of God to help someone focus on the work of God in their life. Even in the storm, the Lord is near, and we can help people best experience the presence of God if we ourselves are prepared spiritually.

Chapter 7

PETER

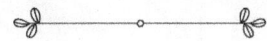

WHY PETER?

Peter the disciple had a strong personality, but he also struggled in the last days of his Lord. He went from being the outspoken disciple to the guy crying in the dark because of his sin.

Peter said that he would die for the Lord (Matt 26:35; Mark 14:31; Luke 22:33; John 13:37), and then he sinned shortly afterward and denied his Lord (Matt 26:69-75; Mark 14:66-72; Luke 22:54-62; John 18:15-18, 25-27).

There's something very important to remember here: Peter failed, but he did not fall away. After he had been restored, he was a man who understood struggle, and he was able to help people in their own struggles.

WHAT DO WE KNOW ABOUT PETER?

Simon Peter was a fisherman and one of the top three in Jesus's inner circle. He was obedient to Jesus's call to leave his nets and follow Him, and he is the one who confessed Jesus as the Christ.

> *15 "But what about you?" he asked. "Who do you say I am?"*
>
> *16 Simon Peter answered, "**You are the Messiah, the Son of the living God.**"*
>
> *17 Jesus replied, "Blessed are you, Simon son of Jonah, for this was not revealed to you by flesh and blood, but by my Father in heaven. 18 And I tell you that you are Peter, and on this rock I will build my church, and the gates of Hades will not overcome it."*
>
> —Matt 16:15-18

Upon that confession—that rock-solid, unwavering confession that Jesus is the Messiah—Jesus would build His church. That same man, in the power of the Holy Spirit, preached a fiery sermon on Pentecost, and the church was born.

Some people may say that Peter only had a setback, or a *lapse in judgment*. The Apostle Peter is a hero among many believers around the world, and it is hard to say that he had a mental health struggle.

"Come on," they might say. "He walked with Jesus! There is no way anyone would have a mental health problem if they walked, in real life, with the Lord." That thought has crossed my mind before too.

Remember, though, that this man—Peter—who walked on the earth with Jesus, also walked on the water with Jesus. Peter had faith that was strong enough to get out of the boat, and everything was cool until he took his eyes off Jesus. Then *the darkness closed in.*

WHAT TRAUMATIC EVENTS LED TO PETER'S MENTAL HEALTH CRISIS?

How would you feel if someone you loved very much told you that they were going to die soon? What would you say?

I would say, "No way. We are going to get the best doctor, or the best lawyer, and we are going to pray and trust the Lord to heal you." That is what I would say, and I have said that. How can someone so healthy, or so good, suffer?

His ways are not our ways.

Matthew 16:21 tells us that after Peter confessed Jesus as Lord, Jesus began to tell the disciples that He was going to Jerusalem to suffer, die, and rise again. I think Peter's crisis began here, before the Garden, when His Lord told them He was on His way to die. The disciples were confused about all of this (Luke 18:34); it was not what they were expecting. Uncertainty about the future can lead to fear, which can lead to anxiety and depression.

After the Last Supper, Jesus took His disciples to the Garden to pray. (Prior to going to the Garden, Jesus had told Peter that he would fall away and deny the Lord. How would all of this weigh on your heart?) The disciples fell asleep in the Garden. *Peter* fell asleep. Was Peter sleeping because of fatigue and stress? They were probably all exhausted mentally *and* physically.

Then came the arrest, and brave Peter the fisherman ran away, along with the others.

> *Then all the disciples deserted him and fled.*
> —Matt 26:56b

Jesus was led from the Garden into the hands of the high priest and into a series of trials. Each of these events pushed Peter deeper into the darkness—until the rooster crowed, and he remembered what Jesus had said.

THE MENTAL HEALTH CRISES OF PETER

Peter's Lord—and Friend—had been arrested. The disciples were afraid, and Peter was afraid. As Jesus was being beaten and questioned, Peter was denying any relationship with the Man whom, hours before, he had told he would die for. Then Jesus looked at Peter:

> [61] *The Lord turned and looked straight at Peter. Then Peter remembered the word the Lord had spoken to him: "Before the rooster crows today, you will disown me three times."* [62] *And he went outside and wept bitterly.*
> —Luke 22:61-62

When Peter remembered what Jesus had said, the floodgates of emotions opened, and he broke—mentally, physically, and spiritually. Peter was afraid, and he was spiritually broken.

Luke 22:62 uses the word *bitterly*. This is more than just crying; this is weeping loudly or violently. In the King James Version, the Greek word is πικρῶς, *pikros*, which means "violent weeping." Suffice it to say, Peter was not in a corner sniffling quietly like a scolded child.

One thing to notice in Peter's brokenness is that he did not seek solitude and go into hiding. He was with the group when the word arrived that the tomb was empty. This is so important. In our own mental health struggles, we need to be *with* people, even when we prefer to be alone. It is important to be with people you love and people who care about you.

We do not know much more about Peter's crisis, but we do know that the Lord restored Peter (John 21:15-17). Then, when the Holy Spirit came to Peter, he was a man on fire for his Lord (Acts 2:14-41).

WHERE DID PETER FIND COMFORT?

Peter found comfort in his restoration.

You may say, *Wait a minute, what?* But follow along with me on the path of his restoration.

First, in his crisis, Peter did not run from the Lord or from the other disciples. He was with them on Resurrection Day, and he was with them on the lake (John 21). Second, the disciples had been fishing all night, and in the morning a man on the beach asked what we all ask people who are fishing: "Hey, catch anything?" (my paraphrase).

> *Then the disciple whom Jesus loved said to Peter, "It is the Lord!" As soon as Simon Peter heard him say, "It is the Lord," he wrapped his outer garment around him (for he had taken it off) and jumped into the water.*
> —John 21:7

When Peter realized that his Lord was near, he did not run and hide in shame as the first man and woman did in the Garden (Gen 3:8). Instead, he jumped into the water to go to Him. As quickly as he could swim, Peter went to His Lord—the only One who could restore him.

Finally, the Lord fed Peter and the others physically before He fed Peter spiritually. Do you remember the word of God to the Prophet Elijah?

> *"Get up and eat, for the journey is too much for you."*
> —1 Kgs 19:7

If you know the plan that the Lord had for Peter, then you know it was too much for him to do on his own. So the Lord restored Peter with three simple questions of, "Do you love me?"

The question is the same for every one of us. *Do I love Jesus more than anything or anyone else?* If the answer is *yes*, then be obedient to what He has called you to do.

However, if the answer is *no*, then what are you going to do about it?

That time on the beach with his Lord brought the healing and restoration that Peter needed to continue in his calling. Because of his failure, his crisis, and his restoration, Peter was able to speak to others who had also denied Jesus.

Acts 3 tells us that Peter and John, through the power of the Holy Spirit, had healed a lame man. This got a lot of people's attention, and Peter confronted them.

> "You **disowned** the Holy and Righteous One and asked that a murderer be released to you."
>
> —Acts 3:14

Peter, the same man who denied, or disowned, Jesus, was now accusing others of the same sin. Peter had been restored, and he knew that others could find restoration.

> [17] "Now, fellow Israelites, **I know that you acted in ignorance**, as did your leaders. [18] But this is how God fulfilled what he had foretold through all the prophets, saying that his Messiah would suffer. [19] **Repent, then, and turn to God**, so that your sins may be wiped out, that times **of refreshing** may come from the Lord, [20] and that he may send the Messiah, who has been appointed for you—even Jesus."
>
> —Acts 3:17-20

Peter had repented and turned to the Lord, and he had been comforted and restored. He was telling the people that they, too, could be restored and their sins could be wiped away. We all need a time of refreshing from the Lord through His forgiveness.

HOW CAN YOU HELP SOMEONE WHO IS STRUGGLING WITH DEPRESSION CONNECTED TO GUILT?

We have asked this question at the end of each chapter, but here, the situation is different. Peter was not depressed because he had lost a loved one, or his life had been threatened, or God had punished him. Peter was depressed because he had failed His Lord whom he loved so much, and he had sinned. How do we help someone in this situation?

This takes spiritual discipline and patience to walk with a brother or sister in Christ in their brokenness, and to be able to help them return to the Lord. I highly recommend getting someone from your church staff involved.

The fallen believer needs to have a level of trust with you before you can lead them to restoration. They may not want to give you a lot of information; it may begin with a simple statement such as, "I feel like I have been backsliding." When I hear something like that, I do not ask questions. In fact, I do not say anything. I allow an uncomfortable silence to develop. Then, if they do not say anything more, I will say, "I would like to pray for you that the Lord Jesus will draw you back to Himself and restore you."

If possible, follow up with the person in a few days—but do not be annoying. (Note: it is best for men to counsel men and women to counsel women.)

Chapter 8

PAUL

WHY PAUL?

We *must* study Paul.

Paul followed Jesus for roughly thirty years, and his Christian life was a life filled with hardship. He travelled thousands of miles with the gospel of Jesus, and it seems that he suffered every step of the way. He was eventually beheaded at the order of Emperor Nero of Rome, according to church historian Eusebius.

WHAT DO WE KNOW ABOUT PAUL?

Paul was born in Tarsus, which today is in Southeastern Türkiye. He was a Hebrew, a Pharisee like his father, and a Roman citizen by birth.

As a Pharisee, he was very zealous for the Law of God, and he did his best to persecute the Jesus cult known as "The Way" (Acts 26:9-11). He worked against the Jesus followers until he met Jesus, and then Paul's life was radically changed.

Paul, who had been a "Hebrew of Hebrews" (Phil 3:5), was hated by his own people who refused his gospel message, and he became the missionary to the Gentiles (Acts 13:46). He took the gospel from Jerusalem to Illyricum (Rom 15:19).

WHAT TRAUMATIC EVENTS LED TO PAUL'S MENTAL HEALTH CRISIS?

> [23b] *I have worked much harder, been in prison more frequently, been flogged more severely, and been exposed to death again and again.* [24] *Five times I received from the Jews the forty lashes minus one.* [25] *Three times I was beaten with rods, once I was pelted with stones, three times I was shipwrecked, I spent a night and a day in the open sea,* [26] *I have been constantly on the move. I have been in danger from rivers, in danger from bandits, in danger from my fellow Jews, in danger from Gentiles; in danger in the city, in danger in the country, in danger at sea; and in danger from false believers.* [27] *I have labored and toiled and have often gone without sleep; I have known hunger and thirst and have often gone without food; I have been cold and naked.*
>
> —2 Cor 11:23b-27

When I read 2 Corinthians and Paul's other letters, I think, *Oh, wow!* Paul must have had some mental health struggles because his physical struggles were unbelievable. These verses in 2 Corinthians 11 are like a highlight reel of personal trauma.

I do not know how I would handle one of these hardships, and I believe I would collapse under more than one.

THE MENTAL HEALTH CRISES OF PAUL

Paul said that he "despaired of life" (2 Cor 1:8). In Paul, we see the common struggle with depression and despair. Was he suicidal? I don't think so, but I believe that he did struggle with depression.

There were times in Paul's journey when he did not want to live anymore, but I do not think he was at the point of taking his own life. Paul knew his calling, and he knew that as long as he was alive, he had work to do. Let's take a look at his letter to the Philippians to support this line of thought:

> [21] *For to me, to live is Christ and to die is gain.* [22] *If I am to go on living in the body, this will mean fruitful labor for me. Yet what shall I choose? I do not know!* [23] *I am torn between the two: I desire to depart and be with Christ, which is better by far;* [24] *but it is more necessary for you that I remain in the body.* [25] *Convinced of this, I know that **I will remain, and I will continue with all of you** for your progress and joy in the faith,*

> *²⁶ so that through my being with you again your boasting in Christ Jesus will abound on account of me.*
>
> —Phil 1:21-26

Knowing God's plan for our lives does not make the suffering any easier to accept, unfortunately—take Jeremiah, for example.

Paul carried a burden for other believers, especially those in the churches he had planted.

> *²⁸ Besides everything else, I face daily the pressure of my concern for all the churches. ²⁹ Who is weak, and I do not feel weak? Who is led into sin, and I do not inwardly burn?*
>
> —2 Cor 11:28-29

In his depression and in his worry for other believers, Paul also found himself alone (except for Luke) in his last days.

> *Only Luke is with me. Get Mark and bring him with you, because he is helpful to me in my ministry.*
>
> —2 Tim 4:11

"Get Mark and bring him with you." Paul longed for companionship. Depression is even harder when you are separated from people you love. I know this feeling after spending a week in prison in another country.[2]

WHERE DID PAUL FIND COMFORT?

Paul's source of comfort and strength was in his Lord.

> [9] *One night the Lord spoke to Paul in a vision: "Do not be afraid; keep on speaking, do not be silent.* [10] *For I am with you, and no one is going to attack and harm you, because I have many people in this city."* [11] *So Paul stayed in Corinth for a year and a half, teaching them the word of God.*
>
> —ACTS 18:9-11

Paul had suffered a lot of abuse in Corinth, and it would have been easy to give up and move on. But the Lord spoke to him and strengthened him.

> [9] *Indeed, we felt we had received the sentence of death. But this happened that we might not rely on ourselves but on God, who raises the dead.* [10] *He has delivered us from such a deadly peril, and he will deliver us again. On him we have set our hope that he will continue to deliver us.*
>
> —2 COR 1:9-10

---

2. April 29, 2017: I was arrested on the Turkish side of the border with Syria. I had unknowingly found myself in a war zone and was subsequently charged with espionage and terrorism. The charges were eventually dropped, and I was accused of missionary activities. It was a dark and lonely time in that prison cell.

Listen to Paul's words in 2 Corinthians 4:7-9:

> [7] *But we have this treasure in jars of clay to show that this all-surpassing power is from God and not from us.* [8] *We are hard pressed on every side, but not crushed; perplexed, but not in despair;* [9] *persecuted, but not abandoned; struck down, but not destroyed.*

In our weakness, in our pain, and in our struggle, we are not alone because God is with us. And, in our struggle, we need to fix our eyes on the One who is our hope:

> [16] *Therefore we do not lose heart. Though outwardly we are wasting away, yet inwardly we are being renewed day by day.* [17] *For our light and momentary troubles are achieving for us an eternal glory that far outweighs them all.* [18] *So we **fix our eyes not on what is seen, but on what is unseen**, since what is seen is temporary, but what is unseen is eternal.*
>
> —2 Cor 4:16-18

HOW CAN YOU HELP SOMEONE WHO IS STRUGGLING WITH DESPAIR AND DEPRESSION?

The only thing that could rescue Paul in times of despair and depression was his faith. This is the only thing that can rescue any one of us in our own time of struggle. So, how do we help people?

Again, be there, be present, and listen. As the Holy Spirit leads you, guide them into the Word of God. If you are talking to an unbeliever, ask them if you can share something from the Bible. If they say *yes*, then help them with words of comfort—a great place for that is in 2 Corinthians 1:3-7.

If they say *no*, then listen to their story without passing judgment. Do not try to answer the "why" questions; just listen. If possible, be available to meet with them again.

Chapter 9

JESUS

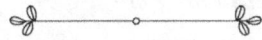

When I first began developing the idea for this book, I had a list of biblical figures I wanted to focus on—including Jesus. However, as I completed the final chapter on the Apostle Paul, I felt conflicted about including Jesus in the same format as the others.

I struggled with the idea of suggesting that the God-Man could experience mental health challenges in the same way we do—it felt borderline blasphemous. After all, the Lord Jesus is the One we turn to in our moments of depression, despair, anxiety, and fear.

I firmly believe that Jesus is both fully God and fully Man (John 1:1, 1:14). In His great love for us, God became like us—yet without sin.

> *⁵ In your relationships with one another, have the same mindset as Christ Jesus:*
>
> *⁶ Who, being in very nature God,*

> *did not consider equality with*
> *God something to be used to his*
> *own advantage;*
> *⁷ rather, he made himself nothing*
>   *by taking the very nature of a servant,*
>   *being made in human likeness.*
> *⁸ And being found in appearance as a man,*
>   *he humbled himself*
>   *by becoming obedient to death—*
>   *even death on a cross!*

—Phil 2:5-8

If Jesus is both fully God and fully Man, and I believe He is, then in His humanity, does He feel what we feel?

The Gospel accounts give us examples of His humanity: He was hungry (Matt 4:2), He was tired (John 4:6), He was thirsty on the cross (John 19:28), He felt sadness (John 11:33-35), He felt anger (Mark 3:5), He felt compassion (Matt 9:36), and He loved (John 11:35). Jesus was like us in every way, but He did not sin. He understood our weaknesses and our griefs, and Jesus Himself experienced grief.

Isaiah foretold the grief the Messiah would feel:

> *He is despised and rejected of men;* **a man of sorrows, and acquainted with grief**: *and we hid as it were our faces from him; he was despised, and we esteemed him not.*

—Isa 53:3 kjv

That prophecy was fulfilled in the Garden.

> *³⁷ He took Peter and the two sons of Zebedee along with him, and he began **to be sorrowful and troubled**. ³⁸ Then he said to them, "**My soul is overwhelmed with sorrow to the point of death**. Stay here and keep watch with me."*
>
> —Matt 26:37-38

The greatest picture we have of Jesus's humanity is in His time in the Garden on the night of His arrest. Matthew tells us that Jesus was "sorrowful and troubled"—the idea of being grieved and distressed. The Greek words used in this passage can also mean "terrified" or "anxious."

The life of Jesus was a constant example of how to be in a right relationship with God the Father. Jesus did not quit, give up, or run away from His mission. He was sent to redeem us, and He did.

> *¹⁴ Therefore, since we have a great high priest who has ascended into heaven, Jesus the Son of God, let us hold firmly to the faith we profess. ¹⁵ For we do not have a high priest who is unable to empathize with our weaknesses, but we have one who has been tempted in every way, just as we are—yet he did not sin. ¹⁶ **Let us then approach God's throne of grace with confidence, so that we may***

> *receive mercy and find grace to help us in our time of need.*
>
> —Heb 4:14-16

In Jesus's grief, He went to His Father in prayer. We should do the same (Matt 26:39, 42). *When the darkness closes in,* we can *approach God's throne of grace with confidence,* and we will receive mercy and the grace we need in our own time of need.

If you do not have this type of relationship with Jesus, if you do not have this confidence to approach His throne, then let me encourage you to cry out to Him. Confess to Jesus that you are living a life outside of His will, and ask Him to save you and restore you to a right relationship with Him.

> *[9] If you declare with your mouth, "Jesus is Lord," and believe in your heart that God raised him from the dead, you will be saved. [10] For it is with your heart that you believe and are justified, and it is with your mouth that you profess your faith and are saved. [11] As Scripture says, "Anyone who believes in him will never be put to shame."*
>
> —Rom 10:9-11

Come to Jesus in faith, and allow the healing to begin.

Chapter 10

PUSH BACK THE DARKNESS

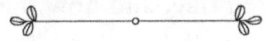

*My comfort in my suffering is this:
Your promise preserves my life.*
—Ps 119:50

In today's vernacular, this book has *wrecked* me! Every section of every chapter has put tears in my eyes. The most difficult chapter for me was Naomi's, and after reading the responses from my friends (Appendix 2), I wanted to quit writing. You do not know someone's pain until you hear their story. Even then, you do not fully understand their darkness.

I have read about these biblical figures many times, but I never really considered their mental health struggles. These men—and Naomi—did great things, and the Lord God used them in mighty ways.

I have learned in a deeper way that all the people we have looked at in this book were regular people—with the exception of Jesus, and He became like us. As noted in the beginning of the book, most people will have some sort of mental health struggle at some point in their life. It may be brief, or it may be prolonged. Your *righteousness* does not prevent you from going through traumatic events or mental health struggles—take Job as an example.

The purpose in writing this book was to look at how believers have struggled mentally for centuries, what that struggle looked like, and how they found comfort. It is my hope that you will find comfort in the same way.

There is a common theme throughout our study, and that is the presence of God in the life of the person who is hurting. Today we have Jesus and the Holy Spirit who is our Comforter, and He understands our pain. Jesus is available, and He is near to the brokenhearted. If you are hurting, if you are in the beginning of a mental health crisis, or if you are deep in the darkness, cry out to Jesus. If you have access to *this* book, you have access to *His* Book.

If you do not know where to begin, begin with prayer. Pray from your heart, openly and honestly, and ask Him to help you. If you do not know where to read in the Bible, turn to the Psalms. You can read some of the verses we looked at in our study of David.

Allow me to lean on the words of our Lord and Savior, Jesus the Messiah. He told us that there would be struggles, and this life is not going to be easy. He also told us that our peace, our comfort, our hope is in Him:

> "I have told you these things, so that in me you may have peace. In this world you will have trouble. But take heart! I have overcome the world."
>
> —JOHN 16:33

You will have trouble in this life, I promise you. In the beginning stages of this book, my mom was dying the slow death of Alzheimer's disease, and she has since passed. During these last few years, I have cried out to the Lord every day for strength, and He supplied my need for each day. I know from experience that when the darkness closes in on me, my comfort is in the Lord Jesus and His Word.

My hope is that you will find that same comfort in the Word of God *When the Darkness Closes In.*

> *You, LORD, keep my lamp burning;*
> *my God turns my darkness into light.*
>
> —PS 18:28

AFTERWORD

I do not know where you are in your spiritual journey. I hope you are a follower of Jesus Christ. If Jesus is not the Lord of your life, I pray that this small book will be the seed that helps to begin a new life for you.

In this life, we will have problems and struggles. However, we do not have to go through them alone. We were created by God the Creator to be in relationship with Him—and with others.

> *"I have told you these things, so that in me you may have peace. In this world you will have trouble. But take heart! I have overcome the world."*
>
> —John 16:33

May you find rest for your soul in Christ Jesus.

APPENDIX 1:

CRISIS RESPONSE NUMBERS AND WEBSITES

If you or anyone you know is struggling with a mental health crisis, please call the number below. The line is open twenty-four hours a day, and you can speak with a trained mental health specialist:

National Hotline for Mental Health and Suicide Prevention:

1-800-273-TALK (8255), or call 988

You can also call the following:

The National Alliance for Mental Health:

1-800-950-6264

For Veterans—Veteran Crisis Line:

1-800-273-8255

Vets for Warriors, a military community serving veterans in crisis 24/7:

1-855-838-8255

For more information on how to talk about suicide, non-suicidal self-injury, and intimate partner violence, go to *jasonfoundation.com*. Education is the key to prevention.

APPENDIX 1

They also have an app called "A Friend Asks." This is a great resource to use if you are concerned about someone.

For information on how to establish a griefshare counseling service for survivors, visit *https://www.griefshare.org/*

For more information on mental health, visit the National Alliance on Mental Illness: *nami.org*

For crisis counseling, text HOME to 741741. You will be connected with a trained, volunteer crisis counselor, and they are available anytime.

APPENDIX 2:

CHRISTIAN RESPONSES TO LOSS OF SPOUSE AND/OR CHILD

It was very difficult for me to ask my friends to respond to these questions. I have heard their stories firsthand, and I have seen their tears. The pain never goes away, but they have learned how to lean on the Lord.

Flip through to read their responses.

APPENDIX 2

REPLY #1

Question	Response
Are you Male or Female?	Female
Do you follow Jesus as your Lord and Savior? If yes, how long have you been saved?	Yes. 52 yrs.
Have you experienced the loss of a spouse, and or child?	Yes
If yes, which, and how long were you together?	Spouse. 38 yrs.
Did you experience a "Mental Health Crisis?"	Yes
If yes, which of the following did you experience?	a. Depression - ✓ b. Loneliness - ✓ c. Survivor Guilt - ✓ d. Bitterness towards the loved one - ✓ e. Bitterness towards God f. Hopelessness: The feeling of I can't go on g. Anxiety or worry about the future - ✓ h. Desire to end your life: The feeling of I'd be better off dead - ✓
Where did you find comfort in the beginning? Where are you finding comfort or peace now?	Family/Prayer/Faith
How can the Faith Family help someone experiencing these crises?	**Show compassion - not just in words but with their time, prayers, and help them become active in helping others.**

APPENDIX 2

REPLY #2

Question	Response
Are you Male or Female?	Female
Do you follow Jesus as your Lord and Savior? If yes, how long have you been saved?	Yes, for 51 years
Have you experienced the loss of a spouse, and or child?	Yes
If yes, which, and how long were you together?	Spouse, almost 24 years married, and almost 1 year dating/engaged
Did you experience a "Mental Health Crisis?"	yes (at times)
If yes, which of the following did you experience?	**a. Depression /** **b. Loneliness /** c. Survivor Guilt **d. Bitterness towards the loved one /** e. Bitterness towards God f. Hopelessness: The feeling of I can't go on g. Anxiety or worry about the future h. Desire to end your life: The feeling of I'd be better off dead
Where did you find comfort in the beginning? Where are you finding comfort or peace now?	My comfort came from God. I'm still finding comfort from God, but my church family and other friends have stepped in to help me.

APPENDIX 2

Question	Response
How can the Faith Family help someone experiencing these crises?	Every case will be different. When it is just husband and wife with no children, you often become best friends sharing everything with each other. Then when one is gone, you have no one to fill in that gap. Friends and family need to step up to the plate and make sure that person gets at least a weekly "touch" from someone. **Loneliness could be detrimental**. If a husband dies, offer to help do things around the house (home repairs, landscaping, etc. that maybe the husband used to do) If a wife dies, maybe the man needs help learning how to cook or do laundry, etc.

REPLY #3

Question	Response
Are you Male or Female?	Male
Do you follow Jesus as your Lord and Savior? If yes, how long have you been saved?	42 years
Have you experienced the loss of a spouse, and or child?	Spouse
If yes, which, and how long were you together?	44 years
Did you experience a "Mental Health Crisis?"	yes

APPENDIX 2

Question	Response
If yes, which of the following did you experience?	Depression, and Loneliness
Where did you find comfort in the beginning? Where are you finding comfort or peace now?	Greifshare counseling at Advent Church. Friends really didn't know how to respond after initial days
How can the Faith Family help someone experiencing these crises?	Establish Greifshare Plan counseling at local churches to serve the community. https://www.griefshare.org/ The biggest problem I had was interacting with others, I didn't have any faith issues. People don't know how to react to you once you are no longer a couple. Doing work with Disaster Relief and ramp building (dealing with men on men) was not much of an issue, but other social occasions were very stressful. Going to church home groups, social celebrations etc... were very difficult. I cried a lot. The grief share program helped me face a lot of these issues. Nowadays the Lord has placed another woman in my life, so most of the depression and loneliness has disappeared.

APPENDIX 2

REPLY #4

Question	Response
Are you Male or Female?	Female
Do you follow Jesus as your Lord and Savior? If yes, how long have you been saved?	Yes, I sure do (Follow Jesus) 33 years
Have you experienced the loss of a spouse, and or child? If yes, which, and how long were you together?	Spouse, my husband passed 2 weeks shy of our 25th anniversary. We dated 1 1/2 years before we married
Did you experience a "Mental Health Crisis?"	Yes (Did you experience a Mental Health Crisis?)
If yes, which of the following did you experience? *(see below)	

I still remember the day just like it was yesterday. Knock on the door and rush to the hospital is when I was asked to show a picture of him. Right then I knew something wasn't right. They took me into a room and sat me down. As soon as I heard we were sorry I went blank. I couldn't tell you anything that was going on. I don't remember coming home. I don't want to talk to no one. Just wanted to left along. I walked in a fog. I felt like my whole world was over. How was I going to live without him? I couldn't tell who all came around. I cannot sleep. I keep waiting for him to come through the door. God should have taken me is what I keep saying because I was the one that was sick and he was right there by my side with doctors and trying to figure out what was going on. Did I miss something, was he sick and I just didn't see it, was I not being a good wife? I distance myself from everyone. I stopped going to church, I wasn't involved in anything. I was so angry with God that I just gave up on everything.

Everything I knew about God's glory, love, eternal life, it went away the day God took him from me. He was a good man, and made me a better person. I gave up because he was everything. I worried about how I was going to pay the bills, fix things that needed to be fixed and just go on living?

My kids, grandkids, family, Church family, and my friends never gave up on me. They were there even when I would lock myself in my room. My kids knew that I would do anything for my grandkids. So, they would say Mamaw I need a hug so I would come out and hold them. They would let me cry if I needed to. People would call or come by and say that God loves you and so do they. They would pray for me and I would just sit and listen.

One day my grandson asked if I was going to come watch him sing at church and I never could say no to them So I did. I sat and listened to the preacher, and it was like a light came on. It was like he was talking to me. My heart just started to beat harder and I started to cry. Before I knew it, I was on my knees asking God to forgive me for running. Forgive me for being angry with Him. When the service was over, I got to talking to the preacher and he explained that God understands and already knew how I was going to grieve. I can now say that God took him because his work here on earth is done and God said, "Well done my child it's time to come and rest." I shared with my family everything and that even though I'm a child of God I even can get lost in this I don't understand.

I can say that God does things that we don't understand. We just have to have the faith that He is right with us and He will never leave us. I know God has a plan for me, and right now I don't know what it is, but in His time I will. I know that I love helping people. I go out with DR and listen to people's stories. Try to do what we can after they have lost everything. I just came back from a DR callout and there was an order that came across to be entered. I just sat there looking at it. I had this feeling that I wanted to go look at the job. So, I asked and we went to look at it. When I got there, I met with the homeowner. We got to talking, and she had just unexpectedly lost her husband just like I did. We had a long talk, and I prayed with her. She felt the same things I felt. It was good to know that there is someone out there that went through the same thing. Then we both asked for forgiveness and just let God take over our lives. WE both are helping-out in church with people, and she is going to get involved with DR where she is from. God uses people in these times to help others out. **God is good, and I might not understand why I can't spend the rest of my life with Shane, but I know now that God has a plan for me, and I'm ready for what He has for me.**

Sorry if this was long but I just went with my heart.

Thank you for asking me to do this.

APPENDIX 2

REPLY #5

Replies 5 and 6 are a husband and wife who lost a daughter during childbirth.

Question	Response
Are you Male or Female?	Male
Do you follow Jesus as your Lord and Savior? If yes, how long have you been saved?	Yes, 32 years
Have you experienced the loss of a spouse, and or child?	Child
If yes, which, and how long were you together?	Died in child birth
Did you experience a "Mental Health Crisis?"	yes
If yes, which of the following did you experience?	Other: **Grief**
Where did you find comfort in the beginning? Where are you finding comfort or peace now?	God is my comfort
How can the Faith Family help someone experiencing these crises?	Just listen, be present, and be a shoulder to lean on

APPENDIX 2

REPLY #6

Replies 5 and 6 are a husband and wife who lost a daughter during childbirth.

Question	Response
Are you Male or Female?	Female
Do you follow Jesus as your Lord and Savior? If yes, how long have you been saved?	Yes, since baptism 71 years ago
Have you experienced the loss of a spouse, and or child?	Child
If yes, which, and how long were you together?	Died in child birth, 3 months early
Did you experience a "Mental Health Crisis?"	**no**
If yes, which of the following did you experience?	
Where did you find comfort in the beginning? Where are you finding comfort or peace now?	I find comfort in my Catholic Faith. I know she is an angel in heaven.
How can the Faith Family help someone experiencing these crises?	Good friends and family prayed for us, and took the time to be with us, individually, and supported us.

APPENDIX 2

REPLY #7

Question	Response
Are you Male or Female?	Female
Do you follow Jesus as your Lord and Savior? If yes, how long have you been saved?	Yes, I do follow Jesus as my Lord and Savior. I have not been baptized yet though.
Have you experienced the loss of a spouse, and or child?	Spouse
If yes, which, and how long were you together?	We were together from 2014 and he passed in July of 2022. We were married September 26th, 2021.
Did you experience a "Mental Health Crisis?"	Yes, I guess you could say that.
If yes, which of the following did you experience?	a. Depression b. Loneliness c. Survivor Guilt d. Bitterness towards the loved one e. Bitterness towards God f. Hopelessness: The feeling of I can't go on g. Anxiety or worry about the future h. Desire to end your life: The feeling of I'd be better off dead ^^**Not really the desire to end my life… just that I would be okay if tomorrow didn't come.**

APPENDIX 2

Question	Response
Where did you find comfort in the beginning? Where are you finding comfort or peace now?	I found comfort with my friends and family. Later, I attended a 10 week class on grief and loss through my church, Hope Presbyterian.
How can the Faith Family help someone experiencing these crises?	The different resources that a lot of churches offer are amazing and very helpful.

REPLY #8

Question	Response
Are you Male or Female?	Male
Do you follow Jesus as your Lord and Savior? If yes, how long have you been saved?	49 years
Have you experienced the loss of a spouse, and or child?	Yes a son
If yes, which, and how long were you together?	A son. Three years ago passed away from Covid He was 28 years old.
Did you experience a "Mental Health Crisis?"	It was and is a crisis that we are walking through. God has been tender in His response to our loss but there have been moments of honest, private expressions of disappointment that the Lord did not respond differently or as we prayed so diligently for.

APPENDIX 2

Question	Response
If yes, which of the following did you experience?	**Some small measure of E,F and H** a. Depression b. Loneliness c. Survivor Guilt d. Bitterness towards the loved one **e. Bitterness towards God** **f. Hopelessness: The feeling of I can't go on** g. Anxiety or worry about the future **h. Desire to end your life: The feeling of I'd be better off dead**
Where did you find comfort in the beginning? Where are you finding comfort or peace now?	Comfort from Scripture, a counselor who cares and knows the names of my children and listens to the story from beginning to end with the good, bad and ugly, and emotionally enters into my pain.
How can the Faith Family help someone experiencing these crises?	I have read several books, A Grief Observed by CS Lewis, and others. Cards, letters and meals from friends and church members.
	Walk beside them long after the funeral. Listen more than you speak. Care even when you think they should be past it. Watch "The Chosen" series with them. It will help them more than everything listed above as they walk through grief. Especially season 3 and 4

MORE BY RICHARD KUENZINGER

I am a Sojourner.

SOJOURNER BIBLE STUDY

Leader's Guide & Student Workbook

The *Sojourner Leader's Guide* is a 52-week journey through the Bible—from Genesis to Revelation—designed to equip leaders to guide others in discovering essential biblical truths centered on Christ. Each lesson includes key teaching points and leader insights, with an emphasis on relying on the Holy Spirit for guidance. A powerful tool to help cultivate a lifelong hunger for God's Word.

MORE BY RICHARD KUENZINGER

The Sojourner Student Workbook is a 52-week Bible study designed for learners of all ages who want to grow in their knowledge and love of Jesus Christ. Spanning Genesis to Revelation, this workbook can be used independently or alongside the *Sojourner Leader's Guide* in a group setting. Each lesson encourages deeper understanding of God's Word and invites students into a lifelong journey of discipleship.

A ROAD LESS TRAVELED: ON BECOMING A MISSIONARY

In this poignant and unflinchingly honest memoir, Richard Kuenzinger charts his journey through heartbreak, addiction, and redemption with raw vulnerability and spiritual insight. From early childhood wounds to the depths of despair and ultimately to freedom in Christ, *A Road Less Traveled* offers a powerful testament to grace and healing.

www.ingramcontent.com/pod-product-compliance
Lightning Source LLC
LaVergne TN
LVHW091310080426
835510LV00007B/444